Pennsylvania Furnace

Pennsylvania Furnace

Julie Swarstad Johnson

Editor's Choice Selection
Unicorn Press First Book Series

UNICORN PRESS   2019   GREENSBORO

First printing

Paper   ISBN 978-0-87775-058-1
Cloth   ISBN 978-0-87775-059-8

COVER IMAGE. "[Arrangement of Specimens],"
Hippolyte Bayard. Cyanotype, ca. 1842. From
*Dessins photographiques sur Papier. Recueil No.
2.* Courtesy the J. Paul Getty Museum.

∞

This book is printed on Mohawk Via,
which is acid-free and meets ANSI
standards for archival permanence.

Unicorn Press
Post Office Box 5523
Greensboro, NC 27435
unicorn-press.org

Distributed to the trade
by Small Press Distribution
of Berkeley, California

For Luke,
Sometimes the nighthawk, sometimes the mesquite

                    to steal away from here
the vain detail I love—a thing bright and shiny
that bears its saving: a thimble, a ring, a needle—
its only eye worn wide, diminishing.

CLAUDIA EMERSON

Pennsylvania Furnace

The Burning World

Undercurrent

Look Back

Pennsylvania Furnace

The Burning World

What the Gaps Reveal at Swatara Furnace

In every cut opened between
    the blocks layered to make
        the high, straight sides
    of this furnace stack—in every

        gap widened as the wooden
    buildings fell away, burned or rotted or
hauled off to raise a barn or house—
    in the waves of moss woven

over smoke stains on the smooth
    angles of these stones—in every
        tiny, shadowed opening along
    the face of this abandoned thing, spiders

        flex, legs limber and loose,
    small bodies visible where the light
trickles in. Before I know their presence,
    I know the stack's shadow

around me: the forest only
    a century old, resurrected
        after the woodcutters turned
    its height into charcoal, into

        smoke settled in the folds
    of children's clothing, into a column
of cloud like God leading his people
    out of Egypt, centered above

the furnace day and night as an exodus
of cooled iron threaded out
between the hills on muleback.
And when the charcoal

or ore veins or business sense
ran out, then the wagons loaded
with earthenware pots, a cast iron
pan, the family Bible turned

for the cities. The last heavy tone
of the casting bell lengthened
in the evening air, shivering
the webs laced between the stones

even then. When I draw closer
to the stack's high sides, when I
step into the casting arch and crouch,
peer up through that opening

once filled with the crucible's
steady heat, I can hear them—
host of silent voices praising every
shadow. I can hear the noiseless song

of the multitude, of the spiders living
on what we left behind, finding use
not in the thing itself, but in what
it opened, the gaps in its story.

Night Watch, Greenwood Furnace

The horses can't read in this hellish light.
Who could, in this red flush at midnight
that seeps in at the edges of dreams,

grown so familiar to the sleepers that it leaves
no impression when they wake. The horses
doze, returned to stalls from harness

and traces, the charcoal wagons emptied,
the ore wagons emptied, the filler
now at the furnace mouth counting measures

to pour down into the heat. He streaks crimson
into the sky as each wheelbarrow load
slides down into the fire, sweat daubing

his shirt onto his back, his handkerchief
to his cheeks: thin divide between his lungs
and hell, between him and a light like Armageddon

beginning in this valley, here along the familiar,
whistling stream. The filler's wife will tell
stories about the light as an old woman living

in a city, will call it bright enough to read a newspaper
at midnight. She never did. She will forget
the sour tang that lingered in her mouth most

mornings. And her husband, the filler, he will die
remembering aloud the night sparks
flew up into the sky and then fell down again

unceasingly, a rain of impossible, unending streaks
so that he knew Satan's armies fought the Lord,
and he threw himself down there beside

the tunnel mouth to pray and cry aloud.
Stars fell through the night, his wife woke
in the morning and called him a fool. The horses

again accepted the harness and traces, the weight
of charcoal and embarrassment, ears pricked
to follow the angels still moving across the valley.

Greener Than

How to explain it, except to say
I couldn't understand how there wasn't
another Ace Hardware until Lewistown,
and Lewistown was an unfathomable name
at the bottom of the mileage signs along one of maybe two
main routes through this central Pennsylvania town.
How to explain, except to say I came
from a place where the big-box stores are legion,
where the Arizona desert was bulldozed over decades
to make mile after mile of intersections
that repeat themselves with only minor variation,
a geography of void and plenty, anything available,
if not at this store, then the next or the next. How to explain,
except to say I thought someone had cut off part
of the sky, what was left a small, drab covering
that had me in tears when the rain didn't stop
for a week. And those hills that they sometimes
called mountains, the trees obscuring everything underneath
into ominous shade. How to explain: when one day
what was at first a bird with a rust-colored chest
bounced through the grass and the word
robin lit up in my brain, some wire falling into place
between description and experience,
the joy of it flashing madly like bulbs
on an old movie theater sign. The local words
ridge and *gap* and *run* became little maps,
rudimentary phrases I could repeat to myself
the way I'd once learned *bongiorno* and *per favore*, beginner words
that could act as charms in a new place,

magic keys that sometimes open doors and sometimes
do nothing at all except give you a reason
to keep on going. *Run* and *ridge* and *gap*:
all that water alive in the landscape, all those strange,
long hills shouldering through the dusk
and the places the water cuts through them,
the highway on stilts high above the houses in gray twilight
and the solitary owl—wild, hurtling form—merging
with the solid absence of the trees.

The Woodcutter

Her hands marked with the darkness left by smoke
from kitchen fires, she takes the ax, the bread,
and soft, white cheese in folds of cloth and heads
into the woods. Her eldest, clothed in calico,
will tend the younger children while
she swings that blade through oak and elm. The hours
fall to the song she hears, low thrum of ax
through air that conjures flour or mackerel, goods
for every cord stacked up. Her muscles knot
with effort, strong enough to down these trees
or darn socks, stitch a quilt to keep out cold.
She warms with every blow. Her body fills
the space between the trees, stretches to meet
the sky she's opened, her children's lifted hands.

The Record Keeper

Each day, I slash through every square across
the blue-lined page to mark our lives passing
in the casting shed or charcoal house. The dates
stacked to the left, the worker's names along
the top encase our hours, ensure our pay.
But to the right, I loose a ragged edge:

> *Stacked coal in coal house*
> *Masons finished work*
> *James Kensal married Margaret Boas*
> *Snow*
> *Balloon ascends from Bellefonte*
> *White broke hand*
> *Rain*
> *Rain*
> *Rain*
> *Rain*
> *All hands at work on dam*
> *Forge idle*
> *Highest water known for years*
> *Joseph Watson buried*
> *Hearth put in*
> *Ore received from Hecla*
> *Furnace blown*

My hand writes it all the same: *Election day*
Sols cabbin burnt Fulton child drowned
Two inches, all I have. Read my words, see
my only act of keeping in a burning world.

What the Susquehanna Tells Me about Blood

Surely the trees still hold the image of my mother's father
moving, paddle in hand through all this shade. The sun
stills above the river, crowns me, returned daughter
in the place her parents left. And look, what summer's done

to make these valleys Eden restored. They never told
me evening was endless, how strawberry scent warms
roadside stands, how the breeze fusses every surface gold.
How all that glint can cover over every loss, transform

it into lit ripples and rocks, a sheen off the water's bulk.
I could drift off on it. Here, on the bridge, time's ignored
for elbows pressed against steel beams, for a soothing sulk
in a story half-known, misremembered, shored up

by longing to know myself, certainty that origin tells
me all I need to know. A trip down the river,
the body cradled by the canoe's tender shell.
The danger in the blood, not the water. Shiver

sent through the body by damaged cells, present
or still years off. The disease has nothing to do
with his trip or this river, but what a form the water's lent
to my unmet grandfather. It's enough, that canoe

clumsily tied to a tree, little boat enough to spark
a world from a remembered sentence: "He floated
the Susquehanna from Sunbury." One remark,
and I can taste the metal's warmth. One drifting boat—

the living body for the dead. The water can tell
me what has stayed unsaid: four teenaged children's grief.
Surely I've heard the date, what it was that attacked his cells,
disaster's pale ghost. But it's become belief:

stilled hospital rooms, absence filling the house, how young
my mother felt, how old the afternoon. I think she must
now love the lap of water on a hull, the hum
a voice makes caught in the hemmed-in space, the slowed thrust

of the river against the bridge, the river against my hands
braced on steel, something more than fruit in the summer air.
The wind reverses course. My little vision withstands
it—no, it's made to drift, made for the river's ceaseless repair.

The Cosmorama Reaches
Hopewell Furnace, 1837

My sister cried as it crept past our cabin.
She couldn't think why a house
would slide by, couldn't see the wheels
that carried it along, rutting the ground
as it passed. From behind, I could see

the narrowness that let it creep
down the road. She stopped crying
when she saw the world contained inside
those thin walls and the windows opening
onto spires and towers in Paris, a billow

of ash above Vesuvius. For an instant,
even I believed myself among the crowd
huddled on the shore, the volcano
burning and raw across the water.
But the brightness never moved

the way the furnace light does, seen
from across the valley. My sister
will join the women in the field next harvest.
The young boys in the blacksmith's shop
will never see France. They beg to give

their wages for the trick of thick glass
and mirrors, the stink of half of Hopewell
pressed in the wagon at once. Two years ago,
I gave my money to hear a traveling lecturer
in a cheap suit, and I learned my money's worth—

a magic lantern to show me manna, golden
circles heaped in the dirt. He never mentioned
the years the Israelites walked or the stiffness
in their shoulders from traveling so long
through heat stifling as the smithy hearth.

And Zion Was Our Mournful Theme

There it was, that Biblical
trouble, that Old Testament debate we'll have
in Sunday School for years: bulbous webs snared
the tips of oak branches along the road and in the woods
behind my apartment, their sick forms devouring
the heights of my joy. I felt the summer
    as a mania,

    as a quivering
in my tendons, at my elbows, behind
my teeth. That green-green (no way but to double
it, that sheer pleasure of multiplying, like some
languages use for the plural) overwhelmed
my desert sensibilities, told me that
    this unfurling

    of surface and color,
could only mean wild goodness, riotous reprieve
from desolation. What wickedness, then, those
webworms seemed, their thick-walled hubs
a curse, a blight, a sty. And worse, their threads'
gossamer beauty, their pale shine littered
    with refuse, dried

    leaves, shattered bark,
and the churning mass alive at the web's center,
a gross, writhing crowd I didn't even wish
to distinguish as individuals. How
close I had to step to try to see them, how
near I came and entered the reek, the sweetness
    they gave off

like apple cores
rotting, bodies of leaves decaying in pooled
rain. How to tell the many from the one, what
to make of God's collective retribution, that ache
in the hymn I love, the story of captivity along
Babylon's river for the sins of the whole.
How I wished to step

back, away from
the pulse of motion in the web. I couldn't
stand, I'm sure, to see blood moving, pumping
through a heart, that tough and necessary muscle
rooted in the chest. Repulsive and gorgeous,
that tint of cells drunk on oxygen, the red-red
saturated

with breath, holy or un-.
All those leaves flushed with sun, fed on the rot
rising from the soil. I couldn't see the single bodies
and the whole body on the same inhale. But I can choose
to call it not ruined. I can say, city beyond my
knowledge, thick light circling in my chest. To myself
I can say, be still.

Team

Pity the mules that labor beneath the sweet,
thin sound of bells. The harness leather dulls
the late morning light even as the bells shine
and glimmer. Pity those mules that

love the weight of the ore, pity yourself
for thinking they might love it, that they
might lull themselves to a trance, ears cupped
to hold in the bell's songs. Pity yourself,

you who hear them as songs. In the wagons,
the earth tries to settle itself back into balance.
It smoothes and soothes itself, it does nothing
but allow gravity in, corrector of all

the upturned, moving things. Corrector
of the men walking beside the mules and their thin,
sweet cries. Correcting the dust in the folds
beside mouth, beside eye, hidden beneath hair.

Can you pity them, you who haven't seen
the road in the moments before the wagons'
rumble turned presence? You who are
and are not earth, you with lungs like silver.

The Storekeeper Serves the Woodcutter

She shuts the door behind her firm as she
heaves an ax through wood. Her voice clips
through the rattle of coffee he pours into bags,
the shush of flour he scoops from bins. She keeps

accounts on a slip of paper, calculates
the pay she earns for every cord, the cost
of all his goods. When her husband died,
he cut the edge off prices to help her buy,

but she saw the difference, her eyes measuring
potatoes and molasses against the trees
she felled. He thinks of her at home, heavy pot
swung from the fire as she pierces a potato,

smoothes a child's hair with her other hand.
She tests them both for softness—what she
wills from the potato and longs to keep
within the child. Some days he smells the oil

from mush fried that morning rising from her
hair, or damp-earth sweat mixing with molasses,
milk gone sour, the flour and egg for rivvels
pressed between her hands. She tells him

about the view from the ridge top, the wind
pulling song from the pines. Her daughter
takes the coffee and bacon wrapped in paper
while she hefts flour back into the sun.

Minnie Gulch, Colorado, July 1998

after Ciaran Berry

Mountain flower pressed in a book. Our tires grinding
          above the cliff face, and in my mind, something
lodged like a half-seen reflection, or a glass bird,
          or water rushing out of sight.

It's all so diaryish, so 24-exposure camera purchased
          for vacation, so snapshot of my family
at the highest pass, the commemorative sign. What I
          believe in: the blueness

fixed in a mass of snow at the peak, a marmot's
          cinnamon bulk in the sunlight, a columbine plucked
from the shade and folded onto itself in the guidebook.
          And what really happened:

my growing desire—good American—to possess
          the narrow canyon, to glide on ore tram wires,
a glass hummingbird on fishing line
          at the tourist shop in Ouray.

Mementos of summer. Same shop, different colors tumbled.
          Stones for children to treasure up in faux velvet
and ribbon drawstrings, manganese and pyrite
          to play at pulling

from the ground. Masking tape can shape an ore crusher from
          wooden blocks, yarn makes a tram wire above the carpet
river and the valley free from toil. Minus the shadow,
          the stamp mill's hulk,

its misremembered, vast inside seen through intact
                    windowpanes, separating the world into what can be
          touched, what can be dreamed. Padlock and chain link,
                    the mine's steep darkness behind a sign

left out of my play gulch along with the fear of the edge,
                    our turn at the jeep road's narrowest, rutted passage,
          grind of the engine strong as the hiss of pine needles
                    filtering the wind. Fear

has everything to do with my dream of diving
                    and diving and diving into some radiant distance,
          some river flowing in the darkness miles beneath my feet.
                    Shade-loving columbine

layered into the book and never seen again. Spun
                    color suspended near my window. Beauty I
          bought. The stream pushes downhill, picks up my child heat,
                    my damp, my seeping breath.

Undercurrent

Reading the Landscape

Don't lose it—the ink line
of Tussey Mountain's height

unspools above this Pennsylvania valley,
a loose wave of attention

pooling from a pen. It flows out
above corn tassels, branching maples,

edges closer to the road you drive
with every quarter mile. Like

a script style whose spindled lines
and whorls the world left behind,

the mountain holds meaning
at bay, keeps you tracing its outline

flickering behind tulip trees, lost
to the curve of the road

across the valley floor. This country
baffles you. The maze of ridges

drinks attention, masks distance,
hems you in and eludes you. But the road

calls you forward. The ridgeline rises
up to meet you just when you thought it gone.

David Ford McFarland's Notes for a Lecture at the Bellefonte Historical Society, 1933

It must seem like impertinence for one
who spent his early years in Kansas far
from the iron industry, who never saw
a cold blast furnace until a third of life
had passed to come to Bellefonte, to try to teach
you anything you don't already know.
But perhaps my foreign eyes can see
what you have grown accustomed to, what you
have overlooked. I saw the stone remains
like lone towers left from fortresses
by the roadside when I arrived in this
valley, and I set to learning their past,
not just in books, but from the aged workers
yet living near the ruins, their knowledge
of the work, of the life around the stack
expiring with them. This history
humbles me: I sense beneath the surface
of this place another world just out of reach.
I feel the ghosts of that age gathered
underground like the helium I found
in gas wells on the Kansas plains, an unlimited
supply if you know where to look.
Gentlemen, remember what you have known
about this country and let your knowledge
bring that history into the light. Seek out
the past—your heritage stands around you,
crying for recognition before it crumbles.

Phoenix, Arizona

I inherited this
sky flushed with depth,
these three hundred days
soaking sunlight each
year. I inherited

this city dropped
between mountains,
lined with asphalt
and empty riverbeds and
seared when the heat

won't cool at night
because that asphalt
exhales it out again.
The night sky I
inherited burns violet,

lit by terra-cotta roofed
suburbs spilling east
with their strip malls and
water lifted miles
by canal. I inherited

the fixed grid of streets
to ground me—numbers
for North-South, names
for East-West, order
learned from my parents

who first visited Phoenix
in July, stepped onto
tarmac pliant with heat
and said *yes, here*. They
adopted this city

so I could breathe
my first air in desert
March when poppies
and globemallow burnish
the mountainsides. From

those heights, I watch
the city I inherited
crush desert, putting greens
like mold spots among all that
stucco, blacktop stretched

between everlasting concrete
sidewalks as people
keep coming like my parents,
drunk on all that
space opening above.

Those people and their
cars spit out the rot-brown
smog I inherited, smog
I rage against from
my own car while

the newscasters chant
heat inversion,
no burn day. I
inherited these unending
loops of freeway

circling farther out
with every new
housing development
tapped into the canals,
inherited this lack

of water and lack
of fear deep enough
to make me act. Phoenix,
I inherited your copper
star at our flag's center,

its fake-metal sheen
just like us. We drink light
and air and hold
it inside. We smolder
with trapped heat.

The Ironmaster's Daughter

I move the cloth with practiced hands, adjust
the cloud-high sleeves, the mounded linen skirts
striped green and yellow, slimming my waist
to match the calls of fashion for this year.
This narrow hall can't hem me in: I swell
to fill its bounds. The porch, the stairs all mime
my clever figure, wide here, small there, each
calculated choice. I aspire to more
than this furnace town. With my city cousins,
I shop and measure, tally pleats, frills, buttonholes,
thumb silk or muslin stretched between my hands.
I savor weft and warp, mark every stitch,
and know its worth—admiring looks. I build
my future on my frame, a master's art.

Gutterman's Clogs

The shoemaker carved brick-thick soles
from hardwood, then tented umber leather
above the front to hold my boots fast.

With the straps hooked behind my heels,
I tread the casting house floor, heat
from the spilling iron on my feet like a warm

stone tucked into my bed. Beneath the clogs:
sand parted in rows to receive
the scorch of metal pooling silver-bright

while I sweat and steam like a draft horse
in the burning air. Last week I dreamt
I walked the casting floor alone, clad

in bare feet. The molten iron flowed out
cool as French Creek in summer,
and I waded into that freshness,

slipping beneath the tymp stone
into the filled crucible to float there
on light that lifted me from this solid ground.

Rivers of Arizona

This story ends in moonlight,
the riverbed flooded with it, a flat glint
off the muddy trickle down the center.
These rivers of my childhood speak
the language of light, midday sun
or moonglow filling them more often
than rainwater which fades out,
dries out, goes underground
into the sandy soil. These rivers
should teach us about borders—they cross
paperless, cottonwoods bursting out,
money-green alongside. Lined in concrete,
my childhood rivers are forced into a channel
so similar to charnel, bone-dry,
pumped, nothing left. When the rivers
flood in Tucson, traffic stops.
I've known women who take their children
to see the water running, muddy
and strong as anything free.
I've known men hunkered in the bushes
upstream from the waste-water recharge plant
shooting ducks, a blue ripple
off a wing now pinned to their wall at home.
Trash traces the lines of the riverbeds.
Thousands of bats bed down beneath a bridge,
at dusk a stream of them curling up like smoke
or like water seeking a path across dry ground.
We'll escape, river to river on a raft,
the German POWs planned. U-boat sailors

shipped to the desert,
a way out
they knew best:
unto water until the sea.
escape the camp. They dug through
they walked through the night
only moonlight
What did they do?
except surrender
the paths of what

they sought
through what they thought
water
And they did
our hard soil,
and found
between the banks.
What do we do
to the light which marks
we crave most.

33

Barn Swallows

Forgive me my transgressions against you,
　　who cross and re-cross the unmown field,

dark constellations forming and breaking,
　　almost nameable, then something beyond memory.

I might have called it joy, the brightness
　　I saw in every shape that afternoon: high summer,

the sun eclipsed to a halo around a caterpillar's
　　furred back, Queen Anne's lace phosphorescent

along the path. Forgive me that I understood it
　　all as a pathway, lit and leading me

to the barn where you nest. I would have
　　assigned the word *expectant* to that dilapidation,

picturesque. You want me closer, I thought. Close
　　enough, and I would transform: pebble heart,

and the wrap-of-wire claws, my joy enough
　　to unfurl feathers. What was my transgression

against you: that I was terrified
　　by your passage in the hot, close air, by what

I understood as your terrified cries? That I returned
　　to the afternoon and you still crossing

and re-crossing the field, everything still lit,
　　and in me, the stone of my anger?

Meditation for Polly

We rehearse Grundman's "The Old Peat Fire Flame"
in municipal band, and although the lilt of piccolos

sounds calculated to make me think of a pleasant flicker

within a stove, instead I think about a peat fire burning
in North Carolina, forty thousand acres smoldering
          on the coast, the ground itself on fire, flames

spreading below the grass the way a high, pink strand
of sky at sunset will smear and shrink, shifting

every moment. Because I have never seen peat,

have only read about the way the fire will sink
beneath the surface, unreachable even just a few feet
          into the ground, I imagine another blaze I know:

the mine fire at Centralia, impossible to extinguish,
burning for fifty years. Someone has studied

the humpback anglerfish drifting in total darkness

a mile deep in the ocean. The Voyager probes
glimmer back at us from beyond the tattered edges
          of the solar system, but we can't halt the spread

of flames underneath our feet, can't bridge that little
distance. When I read in a local history, "Before

they could be married, Polly's skirts caught fire

while she made apple butter, and she burned
to death," I find a gap I cannot cross. I refuse
        to think of her body burning. Such a little

sentence to bear so much weight: the heft of
Polly's skirts or the heavy-handled spoon she grasped

as the smell of apples perfumed the air. Absence

takes her place in the story, like empty streets
in Centralia or a smear of smoke above burning peat,
        ash taste caught on my tongue.

Augury

In the high grass, the rabbit condenses
into the black sphere of an eye, eclipsed

to shadow when his head turns away.
The sky blurs from magenta towards

a darkness deep as that single eye,
and I wait for the opening at the end

of the world, the sudden shading away
that turns what you knew into this gray

whir of twilight where insects click,
heavy in the oaks along the path,

the breeze a motion in the grass,
the rabbit become a stone.

What Gets Preserved

Silk damask curtains block the sun: no
light enters except through shutter crack, glinting off gilded
mirrors and the dimmed eyes of portraits which look
back, dreaming voices. Mansion turned museum,
these halls once held music, not just the dull
green weave across the armchair, the shadows

of clawfoot settees. Over everything, shadows
cast by income, the need for funds. No,
without cash handed in by visitors, the age-dulled
wood of the ironmaster's dining table and this gilded
clock would sit in some attic, no museum
guide to tell their history. I wouldn't look

at them in this guided space now as I looked—
ten years old—at glass cases free from shadow
beneath the high ceilings of the Phoenix Art Museum's
largest exhibit hall. I had seen no
such grand collection before: gilded
sarcophagi, Canopic jars capped with faces dulled

by millennia passed beneath stone. Dull-
eyed students slipped past, not looking
at the alabaster and faience, green gilded
surfaces slick, lustrous. When my shadow
touched the glass case over the mummy, no
hand reached out to terrify me. The museum

stayed quiet like the ironmaster's museum
around me now: vegetable-dyed cloth dulled
with years, dresses and coats sized for struggle, no
toughened frames there to fill them. I look
into the corners. I investigate each shadow
for something solid to the core, not gilded

by imagination, that easily damaged gilt
of what I want to see. This house-museum
preserves nothing but the shadow
of meaning: lists of who worked here, minds dull
with hours in the kitchens, lives spent looking
into the furnace's spilled, silver flames. No

breath, no spark remains preserved. A guilty
image looks from windows of this museum:
the grasping present, wrestling with shadows.

The Unicorn in Captivity

There's a variety of shame called up
by old things——this medieval tapestry,

or handmade quilts' puckered fabrics,
    their less-than-square edges——

  and the humanness they betray.
I've lain awake under hand-stitched sprigs,
    their sagging French knots

a little too close in the dark.

    The human-eyed, rainbow-maned
unicorns of my childhood

prove it: imperfect means indecent. Slick-
    breasted and long-haired,

  those unicorns are so sweet. Not so,
the goat creature in the tapestry's center. Not so
    his eyes, or more properly its——

not superhuman or sub-, but wholly

    other. Fetid and wild, the unicorn
is most like a mule deer passing

through a clearing, sandy body
    suited to the slab head

and motionless eyes. Muscled.
Ungainly. It slips or crashes. It turns
          into a tree at my slightest breath.

The unicorn, even collared and penned,

          looks out at me surrounded
by the symbols of fertility,

patterned flowers frothing over,
          echo of the wire hair

and muscle of the beast. I want to write
that the unknown, the wild,
          the eternal looks out

from the unicorn's eyes. Look at what

          my hands have made: dropped
stitches in the middle of a crocheted

blanket for a child, a ragged
          garden where nothing grows

unless I ignore it. Volunteer plants
turn my yard into the tapestry's swirl
          of greenery, alive in the wind.

Tomorrow, I'll tear them up by the handful.

Passage

The river has picked itself up, walked up
into the sky with feet that crush
the oaks and white pines against the ridges.
The river in the sky wants to unlatch
every window. It feels itself slowed there,
turned to glass. It remembers the riverbed
crush of sand and pebbles rolling along
against its electric skin. The river shakes
open the air, a horse through with the mud
on its flanks, heaving off every clinging
thickness it has passed through. In the sky,
the river breaks open the ridges,
cuts gaps from this world to the next.
All our ghosts move along the valley
in the living river, all our houses
give way to their remembered hands
again on the doors, the basement walls. The sky,
a river, has reached the charcoal flat,
perfect, rounded scar in the woods,
and just another ridge away, the old growth.
A hornet's nest has brought it
to this encircled openness, the vaulted space
shaped by the rain scissoring the canopy.
Spirit lantern, lit but caught—the hornets
gone, for years, the nest a closed world still.

Look Back

Annie Elliot Leaves Centre Furnace, 1851

They make any excuse to miss our prayer meetings.
These backsliders take a warm day to invent work
or a cold to mean impediment, any turn
in the air reason to look back. In two years

of fellowship among their cabins, I've learned
not to blame them. When the sun
colors snow on the mountain the exact blush
of a summer peach, who wouldn't stop

to feel that same light across their cheeks?
In Sunday School, I see the mud
blooming on the women's skirt hems and think
of the gray daub of mold on a glove I left

too long in a dark drawer. I feel the same
patterns spreading in my chest because
of this place, something I know should be washed
away, but with a weird fruitfulness

all its own, a beauty in the way it grows
from what's been given. When I think
of our leave-taking tomorrow, Mr. Elliot
called on, I feel barren. We must

obey. I have formed attachments—
to these women, to even their eyes
hard as the rock hauled up from the ore banks.
We will leave with the air

sharp and thin around us, a proof
that harshness breeds splendor, the cold
a vessel to carry sound across miles,
a bell ringing us down the valley.

Watershed

Faith, I might say, is mostly a choice,
but what I really mean is that I know Elk Creek

flows into other creeks, which then flow into
the Susquehanna River, then the Chesapeake Bay,

which I've never seen, so I can't describe
firsthand the dwindling oyster beds I've read about,

although I can imagine the murky water, the oysters'
filtering suck slowed from a week to a year.

I might try to tell you about the coldness of the water
where we swam under the old train bridge across Elk Creek,

or the perfect wide flatness of the stones upstream
where we basked in the middle, together or alone,

or about the mud that got on my shoes when we left
or the poison ivy I avoided as we inched up the bank

and stopped on the bridge to look at the light
touching the boulders on top of the ridgeline,

but what I mean is that a snake swam past us
there in the water, and only one person noticed.

I go back there, to the sun and the wooden trestles,
to the good poems we read aloud then or soon after,

and I don't imagine there's anything more
to the creek than that stretch near Coburn,

that there might be anything better than our unknowing
choice to follow the one who saw the snake.

Final Descent into Phoenix

I could believe the world broke along straight lines.
How could I not after seeing—full night—
my home from above, city where every light shines.

My life's pattern: the square intersection defines
the grid of streets; the streets, my line of sight.
My eyes learned the world broke along straight lines

of subdivision and future subdivision, signs
clustered (*From the low $300s!*) close, despite
foreclosed homes where nothing ever shines.

I have believed this place is hell, the mines
and dams churning unseen, the Salt River a site
for drunkenness, sharp glass, staggering lines

for lost-key locksmiths. I'd swear this city resigns
itself from history for the love of freeways, for the fight
to be first in enjoying *now*, moment where light shines

to erase the darkness, and I love to see it, signs
and streetlights glittering orange beneath me, candle-bright
and inviting, brake lights leading me in straight lines
home—city that consumes itself, city that even still shines.

Magicicada septendecim

Hold until the ground
warms to reach
your heart, that inmost stone
around which you
have grown. Each layered
thought, each hour
you let what surrounds you
remain beyond, adds
luster to your skin, shine
to those diaphanous
wings which lengthen
year by year in the dark.
You remain apart and
the little motions
of growing heat number
the days until no
more preparation
waits, and what next—
if I could shed myself
the way I saw you do, I would.
Risen from the earth,
legs twined to a stalk
green with the fullest flush
of June, you pushed
and slit your skin open,
your body unfurling out slick
with wings pale as a glass
just filled with wine.
Your larger self

shivered out, equipped
for making—song
or children, both a means
of setting something ringing
in the air. You leave
that shell fine as rice paper,
each joint and folded layer
intact, to prove what
you've chosen, a sign
stern as Lot's wife turned to salt.
It will lead you out, that
stillness—strangest violence—
out past that tensed
form you can't help
but imagine might reach
to you at any second.

Eli Bowen Addresses His Reader, 1852

Do not overlook this nation's wonders:
Penn's woods offer beauty and history
to match old Europe's fame. My guidebook
shows the way from Philadelphia to Pittsburgh,
across the Schuylkill, Susquehanna,
Juniata, Allegheny, along the tracks
forged of Pennsylvania iron, molded in flames
which leap from furnace tops across our land.
We lead the world in iron—the world,
not just the bounds of the Union—
sending forth more than Britain or France.
Even Russia cannot produce that glowing stream
which turns to gold as we do. Do not forget
the grace which formed this commonwealth,
Penn's treaty with the Indians, our freedom
to worship, whether in the simple outline
of a Friends' meeting-house, or in the frugal
bareness of the Seventh-day Baptist's cell.
Have you, reader, seen those holy spaces,
seen their simplicity, their frugal use
of wood and air? Penn's Woods teem
with their equals in dedication to good use, to stewardship
of what we have been given. Our mechanical
and mineral wonders secure our fame:
who could see the coal coming forth and not
feel moved by that unseen time, that compressed,
latent life buried deep, pushed up by the pressure
of plates, the earth's movement? Traveler,
do not pass beyond our borders without

learning to name that taste hovering in the air.
We earn the pitch-pine-and-coal tang of plenty
through struggle, through our iron pledge to shape
those things Providence has placed in our care.

A Brief History of Illumination by Gas Lamp

In the gas lamp's flare, the child leans over paper, neck
  crooked like a stalk of Queen Anne's lace weighted
   by blossoms. 1806, and the lamplight cuts

through former darkness—Manchester's thoroughfares
  bloom brilliant with the yellow glow of gas,
   warm haze vanquishing night in the factories

that now weave cotton cloth even in the hollow
  between midnight and dawn. Poorer children stoop
   to gather cotton tufts settling like snow

beneath the spinning mules, diving in and out
  small as sparrows when the frames pull open and
   slam home. Thunder from the flywheels echoes

even beyond the factory walls and the darkness
  hums with sound and diffuse light. Two hundred
   years later, I hang blankets across my windows

at night, doubling curtains to dampen the electric glow
  hovering over the sidewalk. From space, a satellite
   captures the orange flutter, city-sized, on the plains

of North Dakota, where oil companies burn off
  natural gas, enough to heat a half-million houses.
   The oil pays—cheaper to flood the sky

with those gas flares than to pipe it across the prairie.
  That light spreads everywhere, bleeding like dye from
   the cotton mills that colored Manchester's rivers violet.

The Ironmaster's Daughter Watches
Her Husband's Furnace Blow Out

The saffron stripes on the gown fade to gray
as I shut the lid. The china's packed in straw,
the silver fitted neatly in its case.
He's not to blame. The new ways don't work,
too much cost to make anthracite pay. The old—
a dying animal chained to ragged hillsides.
The children can forget all, small mercy.
I'll settle them in the house, the city's
noise my prize at last. I've heard the wagons
begin to go, heard old Moll cry as she left
her house along the bank. I heard someone sing.
Wouldn't I? The hours I'll leave here
between the ridges, those orange auroras
all woke me, breathless, in the darkness.

Voluntary Remediation

My great-grandparents' garage folds itself
flat as a sheet. That garage at the patch
folds itself neat into a suitcase and walks away
while the house and everything else

go to hell. In my dream, the house at the coal patch
sinks into the ground while the raw-sided
ridges sprout backhoes, crushed earth
opening up, sliding into the valleys that deepen

into pits obscured behind oak trees. I can't recall
their names, those mountains or my mine boss
great-grandfather. I can't recall what year coal production
ceased in Mount Carmel, or if it has. At what distance

does a dream become memory, at what depth
does memory stop its slow seepage through
the soil? At what depth does contamination
cease to linger, not of dreams but of acid rain

from the smelters outside Bisbee, another
mine town I want to love? It's settled—my love
or arsenic—among desert tree roots, slenderest
highways. At what depth does home cease,

does a yard exceed the requirements for voluntary
soil remediation, for teams of men who truck in
from El Paso to dig up and replace beloved
shrubs, flowers, property value? On average,

a foot. Backhoes scrape out and change,
the shallow ground as easy to move in Arizona
as Pennsylvania, a yard as simple to replace
as a company-owned house. Sunlight

can look so cheerful on the hood of a clean
white pickup. I can believe the men are honest
who dig up and replace the yards, who have hauled
entire houses across Bisbee to save them

from the widened pit. I can believe they saved
that sky-blue garage. My dreams, like hands
cupping creek water, have held the streets' slope
past Mount Carmel's firehouse, the light flaking metallic off

a bridge leading into that town we've almost all left. The coal-
colored dirt, the rust-blooded copper dirt, the two-lane
curving outside Mount Carmel or outside Bisbee blur
through my dreams, alongside that first shock, the deep

time of the earth opened up, turned up
iridescent, turned up putrid. Through it all,
a shovel blade goes on searching, goes on toward
the edge, that fault line, humming, beneath my nights.

The Clay Pot's Baptism

To make use of you, to make you something

that will hold water and withstand heat, they

entomb you. Stacked above the wood dried

to the whisper and crack of kindling,

you shudder as the bricks settle into place,

edge nestled on edge, blocking out the sky

with rasp and grit. You have dried to leather

through days spent in air, but now you must

gasp in darkness. You wait for the spark

that will turn you to glass with sudden heat.

Praise that flood of warmth, the streaming fire

blue as chicory flowers glimpsed in the yard

when they walled you in. You saw those blue

lions shaking off the air, their mouths

open, breathing out the summer heat.

Even These Things Will Pass Away

Beside the highway, a bird descends.
Wait—beside me, outside the glass, a raven
pulls air over its back, its body slender
and swift as the light coiling back
behind the mountains. Wait—the raven's
body is heavy as the water underground
that the pecan grove can't help but pull
across the desert. Broad-leafed green
erupts from the ranks and rows,
irrigation water flaring with amber light
caught beneath. Like God
at the beginning, the pecan trees
divide water from water, a new expanse
of heaven dotted with sweetness
in their arms. Yes—I am worried
over the coming world. Somewhere, someone
consults figures of groundwater, river water,
average rainfall to approve
a new water line to the groves. Yes—
I anticipate the warm, sweet nut
weighing on my tongue. The light
slides away, the raven descends
over the desert, over the grove, even over
the high, cool mountains. Yes,
the night—yes, the coming night can resolve
itself into this. The bird's body
descends, claws outstretched
now, hovering in that instant
above the road, above the world
that draws away from it so steadily.

Annie Elliot on the River

I've given my life over to motion. I feel it
as the break of water around our hull,
around my hands, around the bodies of trees
bound together at the river's edge. The men

with saws surely feel it too. I can tell
by the way they pull and pull without ceasing
until the whole world becomes sound
and echo you could lose yourself in. We have

left everything, again. We are wanderers
outside the promised land, and I feel I have
not religion enough to overcome
all these difficulties. And yet this evening

is delightful, husband—what else could I say to you?
That the long, laid-out lines of those trees
fill me with both wonder and an ache,
with joy at the works of Nature and men,

with longing for a calmed moment when no work
must be finished? That I wish the wind over the river
would never cease to pull and pull the sky
down around us? I forget the color

of your eyes most days. I celebrated
our second wedding anniversary by breathing
feathers, stuffing ticks for beds, for pillows,
for bolsters. That cloud of feathers circled me,

that cloud enfolded my ceaselessly moving
hands, making a little world. Do you know
I circle in the same way for you? For the ink stroke
of your back as you write sermons,

for the dark cloth of your coat and your
unyielding *yes* to all that is asked of you.
Your hand drifts across my back, our boat
on the river's current. We have left everything

and come to this. A man's voice rises warm
as spices across the water. Those trees could be
cedars for the temple. Our boat, the Ark of the Covenant,
a swaying, golden weight just outside Zion.

Fidelity

Dusk. A nighthawk. A mesquite.
　　Something unseen. The bird skims
　　　　and dives across the surface of the tree,

　　circling up and over, slipping
above each branch's bend, every fluttering

jut of leaves. The tree a silhouette,
　　the nighthawk a living shadow except
　　　　its wingtips, those white bands tracing fire

　　around the tree crown until an electric
afterimage hovers in the air. There's a space

inside the mesquite that the nighthawk
　　never touches, an interior architecture
　　　　of trunk and air. There's a distance

　　the mesquite can't reach where the bird rests,
hidden, cryptic among rocks in the daylight.

What is a marriage but this? Insects
　　rise from the tree's moving arms,
　　　　and the nighthawk feeds on them, submitting

　　itself to follow that beloved shape.
The tree grows radiant, its surface stretching

out, ribboned by the motion of the bird.
　　How they circle one another. How alive
　　　　that form they sculpt into the evening air.

Tell Me about Your Thirst

The Good Year

after Maggie Anderson

That was the year I found webs
bridging roof and power line, mesquite branch
and brick, filigree across every
open space on my porch. And all those spiders,
so delicate among the strands, wincing back,
nervous, timorous at the slam
the screen door makes. That year, back
in the desert, I rushed to a job I almost
quit weekly while the sky grew wider
and emptier every month: vast,
shallow plane like the shore-end of the ocean,
but pinned in place, every shiver
restrained. At nineteen, on a beach,
I had discovered that black
band on the horizon at nightfall,
when ocean and sky blur into
the deepest intimation of emptiness.
It opens so unexpectedly, that possibility
of no satisfaction. Ahead, in that flat year
alone in an office in Tucson, that year—instead
of wildfire—green flushed the mountainsides,
outrageous, weird blush applied too enthusiastically.
And the color: hue of a dry country,
in which the eye perceives something
held back, some wavelength suppressed
or greyed out, but what remains turns
brilliant, translucent, lit
from the inside, stained glass seen
for the first time in darkness,
coloring the night even when I look away.

Black Walnut

In hard times, turn to something
harder—nut you must smash
between stones or strike with a hammer,
stubborn in its will to remain intact.
Turn to it while the states war:
find, in the hull folded tight as hill and hollow,
the makings for home-dyed colors
mastered in recipes women prize,
each an alchemist certain she knows
the perfect proportions to arrive at
brown, drab, dove, hues suitable
for the Confederate soldier.
Pair these colors with a musket
and head for the battlefield, which asks
hardness of you at Manassas, where
Jackson commands you
to "yell like furies," to conjure up
your double in sound to turn
the Army of Northeastern Virginia back.
Your scream terrifies the wealthy Northerners
who watch downriver with picnic baskets,
top hats, yards of fabric flowing over hoop skirts—
all come for Sunday lunch to see an easy win.
They throw themselves into carriages, palms damp
with what your voice conjures up.
Reporters will write you into the papers,
Yankee ink immortalizing you, the home-dyed
mob victorious against the odds. They will
try to spell it, to describe it—"a fox-hunt yip

mixed up with a banshee squall," "a peculiar
corkscrew sensation that went up
your spine"—but will remain unsatisfied
until your yell finally gets recorded
seventy-five years after Gettysburg. The few
of you remaining, living on into
your ninth decade, you will scream
for the microphones, allow your faces
as well as your voices to be captured
in a newsreel. Get the yell exactly right,
the men behind the cameras will think.
Collect it, tag it, file it into the museum.
They forgot the home-dyed cloth surrounding
those shouting bodies in battle, forgot
the black walnuts smashed open, their
riddled, pitted centers broken out
from rigid hulls. They forgot that what
we call history is the walnut's
creased insides and the water boiled
with them to make dye, the creek
that water came from, where little
currents move, each at their own speed,
a tangle of many voices carried downstream.

Fieldwork

Not the sun, but the wind reveals this place,
drawing in a vulture who spins and circles,
who shakes up the weeds until the sound
of sewing machines ghosts the air. Women
hunch at the machines, feeding in the fabric
inch by inch for slips and peignoirs. The gravel

is sharp enough to cut where it's hidden
under tough stems, chicory a heady flourish
across the empty lot. The vulture's
so low, I taste salt as it passes. Finer
than viscose and polyester, its wingtips
slip the air's feed dogs, the afternoon

stuttering over the threads the vulture
pulls from the sky's weave. The lot is empty,
the lingerie factory gone for decades,
the bridge over the creek beyond trimmed out,
its road erased. I know it by the piers
still sunk under the water. The current

spins there, caught on the broken concrete.
I float on the top, worrying over leeches,
broken needles, sharp-edged cans—the past's
every little disappointment. And what else
would we do with them? Leaves flash brighter
than stars on the creek's surface, the water

wholesome as any weed, sweet and damaged
as their flowers crushed underfoot. I cut
across, against the current, in love
with the speckled shade, the water
spotted like dirty glass and just as cool.
But even the sweep of my arms pushes

against those hidden piers, everything breaking
over what's already broken, turning back
and pushing on again. Speckled and spotted
with the blue stars of chicory, the lot
crashes over and against itself, moving backwards
against time: the women work that same

circle of hem forever, the vulture cuts around
to begin another and another pass. Then,
it dips a wing. It sails out above the creek, going.

The Ironmaster's Daughter Takes Her Granddaughter to the Opening of the Philadelphia Zoological Gardens, 1874

In my grasp, Clara's hand slips and tugs by turns,
her pulse as quick as the music swelling from
the mouths of horns and cornets arced around
the lions—bronze—that crouch among the crowd.
My Clara lifts her hem when I lift mine,
her slim-cut sleeves and bustled skirts a flame
of amber, crimson. At her wrists, fine velvet black
as charcoal, not the pale linen I wore
at ten, the furnace smoke beat out in the wash.
We pause beside the tiger, watch her mark
her world in measured steps. I know her look,
know Clara's eyes reflect this crowd, the streets
we traced to reach these bars. She points to flags
snapping. I feel the tiger's waiting breath.

I Lift Up My Eyes

Don't trust a wet year. What a thrill
   you feel when the front range turns up
glowing one day, lit with green across the peaks
   and high passes. From the desert floor, plants
     and rock might as well be one, everything

budding out from the glut of water,
   from the stored pleasure of wind and rain
all the spring afternoons. The mountains might never
   look so full as they do now (full as in

brimful, fraction away from outpouring,
   the body unmaking itself in grief, the body
unmaking itself in joy, the spirit hovering
   over the body's waters). Now: the beginning
     of dry foresummer, that dangerous season

when heat seems to rise up from the ground, when
   wildfire might raze the mountain down
to sharp edge and blackened pines, a threat
   every dry year heightens. Now, you turn to praise

the fullness of a desert mountain turned green, and
   against that fullness, a column of smoke—
you see it in the afternoon and stop, watch
   the gray seep across the cloudless sky.
     There—after dark, you spot the fire filling

a canyon (brimful still, mere moments
    away from outpouring). You see it from the west,
that canyon you've never been able to distinguish
    before this moment with fire tracing

its outline. Flames move over every angle,
    flaring above every hidden edge made hypnotic
and unbearable. Flames move, and you think:
    lovingly. The mountains might never look
        so beautiful as they do tonight,

on fire. You drive home, descending from the foothills,
    the flames pulling your eyes to the mirrors,
over your shoulder with every turn (with love, that full
    attention). Free and moving fast, the fire

advances to meet you, you believe. But deep
    in the city, from your little hilltop home, you can see
the gulf between the fire and the city lights.
    From here, that blaze becomes a glow,
        a scatter of red and amber flashes

miles upslope from the furthest homes or roads.
    By morning, it's gone. Low temperature,
fast burning, you read, a healthy, low-grade fever
    fed on all that sweet, new growth, a flash

sweeping over steepness and gone. Gone, thank God,
    you think. A miracle. You could have
craned towards it, against the patio door's
    coolness all night. Sweet wildness,
        you whispered. Dear, unforgiving heat.

Lighter

Dust sparks
the air over the flats—
      motes gentle
slowing the light
rosing every edge.
        Desire: leave the car
and walk—roadless
soundless through barbed wire
floating across hollowed
        hallowed washes.
Belief: because the world
ends with the mountains
      the sunset seeps
up through veins
in the bedrock. Traceless.
      At a touch,
I could be set in motion.

She Dreams about the Exodus

Best day ever, everyone sent home from work by lunchtime
because of the ants. They poured out of the vents, dropped
around the edges of the ceiling tiles. Glossy black with
plastic-wrap wings. "Oh, but the West—will anyone want to
live there in twenty years when the water's run out?" Tell me
about your thirst, and I'll tell you about mine. We had been
talking about high desert magic: the way light bleeds away at
evening, the wind-lengthened lines of plants, the watercolor
gradations of distance. Would I give it up? The ants ended
up in drawers, in boxes of paper, behind every desk leg, in
the corners of the lunchroom. Nothing to do but wait for
them to die, the mating swarm mobbing our vents by mistake,
maybe drawn to the water pooled on our roof from the
monsoon the night before. They're looking for a damp place,
the pest control people said. A new colony. The monsoons
seemed changed when I moved back to Arizona. Less wind-
borne dust. Less Biblical plague. When God told Moses and
Aaron to turn the dust into gnats, what did the dust think?
Nowhere damp to go, their shimmering little wings forgotten,
every ant nearly dead by the time they poured down into
our office. Afterward, I saw globules of ants churning above
the sidewalk on muggy summer mornings, shapeshifting
like soap bubbles. Tell me about your thirst, and I'll tell you
about the ants. Someone vacuumed up the piles. Dark little
granules of earth stuck in the overhead lights ever after.

Clara Visits Her Cousins, 1882

My clothing reeks, sooty as the air that stalls
above this porch. In Philadelphia,
the newspaper office glows with Edison's bulbs
while here the furnace burns off charcoal smoke,
and only kerosene lights their rooms. We sit
on the porch—new addition, my cousins' pride—
and I think of our new City Hall rising up
to set world records. They eye my clothes, they talk
of waltzing in Bellefonte. Lamps begin to glow
behind curtains across the stream. The dark
slows my cousins' chatter, and I hear the click
of insects, foreign as this valley, strange
as the roads glinting blue with furnace slag,
the only brightness Grandmother left behind.

Waiting for the Bridegroom

Oak leaves tat the light into lace,
the wind a shuttle that works out the pattern,
lays down its figures on the gravel path

leading back to the cemetery. Maybe
they wore gowns edged in lace fine as light
through leaves, the women ASLEEP IN JESUS

beneath those old stones, maybe too
the infants under tiny markers, only a patina
left on the granite. The chapel beside them

wears the light on its siding as I step inside,
door unlocked and windows shuttered,
the sanctuary a figured darkness. I think

of them risen from their rows in the field
into these ranks of pews, women and children
dressed plainly, no lace, men in somber coats,

the families of this eastern hollow unwinding
their voices in a hymn, a throaty presence
hovering just beneath the ceiling. Alone,

I flip pages looking for words I know
and whistle a tune that looks familiar,
trying to stay calm while I wait

for the arrival of the footsteps I've heard
on the porch since I sat down. I can't
judge their distance over the hum

of heartbeats, the pulse in my ear. Of course,
no one comes, no spirit or living person
bursts in upon me today, in a chapel not really

too far distant from tourists in a potter's studio,
steamrollers repaving the main county highway.
Still, the gravestones and oaks

and I wait, breath held for the Bridegroom
as the dappled light covers everything,
the world seen through some thin veil.

Wonder

The fighter jets have finished passing. I hear the bees again.
The bees have opened everything: yellow creosote buds

and globemallow, the strange blossoms of aloes
    clustered like coral beads on high stalks. I have lived

        in the flight path of the jets and bombers long enough
to let myself forget them. Good bees, they move in the yard,

opening up the jojoba's silver-edged green, the blue-white
    green of Texas ranger leaves, new-mesquite-growth green,

        which is to say green the sun shines through,
green from out of a clear sky. The sun is blocked

by a towhee's passage. The bees have opened
    me to the scarlet cap of a gila woodpecker, the scarlet

        throats of house finches, a cardinal's scarlet call
across a parking lot—a sound that I can't remember as soon

as the air has emptied of it. I might write *shame* for forgetting
    the bombers and the jets. I might write *shame*

        for not dreaming their sound at night, real sound
that could keep me on the edge of sleep, while the flowers

and buds close against me and the darkness.
    Good bees, I don't know where you go in the darkness.

Good bees, good like Christ whom I confess
comes from the Father, but where is the Father?

Goodness reels itself back into strange hives and holes.
    I search the yard. The air never empties of their passage.

Jumping the Pit, Hopewell Furnace, 1936

from the photograph of the same title by Jackson Kemper

He grasps the shovel like a divining rod.
I saw it as the image coalesced in the darkroom,
only distance proving his skill more
than skill, elevating it to magic

vanished from the world. In my photograph,
Lafayette Houck stands transfigured,
feet rooted in the mound of smoking charcoal
twice his height, a shovel held out

before him to balance his body, tune it
to sense the gaps grown as the wood burns away
within the pile. His muscles tense
for flight, to jump and pack down the heap

and keep the flames from erasing the work
that meant his pay. I lived with him
beside that pit for weeks in a hut we built
ourselves, oak leaves and topsoil layered

over boards to keep us warm during the little hours
given to sleep. How could I know, as we built
that hut at the beginning, that the knowledge
of the smoldering wood would fill my mind,

transform Houck and I into mystics, hermits
settled in the woods to learn the ways of fire?
The Park Service sent me—fifty years since
Hopewell lit the sky at night and Houck

learned his trade from his father—*so accurate*
textual and photographic data could be
obtained for permanent record. With pen
and camera, they sent me to save Houck's knowledge

from his aging limbs. While he worked,
I scribbled words—*billets, lap-wood, fagan, reel*—
not knowing those words held power only
as an incantation set to the smell of pitch tar

filling the camp. When the mound charred down
to its base, when the days of watching and tending
at last ended, Houck raked the charcoal out, his gold
produced from base metals steaming in the sun.

No teamster and wagon came to take it.
We abandoned the hut.

Self-Portrait with Tucson

"This is the way we begin and end things."
OFELIA ZEPEDA

One day I saw the mountain of God
        descending across the valley. Sunlight alive

in the body of snow, stepping through the veins
        of ponderosa and granite, cracking the air

balanced between. Valley in my mouth
        when I mean city, when I should say

brick, tile, wash with abandoned couch,
        ocean always just beyond sight, power

lines crossing between that mountain
        and me. You should know I am a woman

who believes in visions. Uncurtained glass
        after sunset, a mirror and the cooled, vast

ceilings it harbors, certainty of memory
        that wakes me in the salt light before daybreak.

By the road, a man shapes circles that connect
        mouth and stomach, prophet's unwashed

hair and empty bag. We are not coming
        to a mountain of fear but a mountain

of joy, a place sweet and yellow as San Xavier
    watermelon. I did not know myself

when I returned home from my long journey.
    Sometimes I see the Lord's mountain

electric pink and close in the rearview, and I know
    there is still a little bit of night left in me.

Notes

The epigraph comes from Claudia Emerson's "Inheritance," published in *Pharaoh, Pharaoh* (LSU Press, 1997).

"The Record Keeper" : The italicized material comes from the Eagle Ironworks record books for 1822-1848 as reproduced in Mary Frances Ward's *The Durable People: The Community Life of Curtin Village Workers, 1810-1922* (Roland Curtin Foundation, 1987) and from the Centre Furnace time book for 1836-1845, housed in the Penn State Historical Collections and Labor Archives.

"The Cosmorama Reaches Hopewell Furnace, 1837" portrays an event described by Joseph E. Walker in *Hopewell Village: The Dynamics of a Nineteenth Century Iron-Making Community* (University of Pennsylvania Press, 1966, reprinted by Eastern National, 2000).

"David Ford McFarland's Notes for a Lecture at the Bellefonte Historical Society, 1933" draws from a document found in the David Ford McFarland Papers and Pennsylvania Iron Furnace Collection in the Penn State Historical Collections and Labor Archives.

"Meditation for Polly" : The quoted material comes from Mary Frances Ward's *The Durable People: The Community Life of Curtin Village Workers, 1810-1922* (Roland Curtin Foundation, 1987).

"Annie Elliot Leaves Centre Furnace, 1851" and "Annie Elliot on the River" both draw from Annie Elliot's 1851 diary housed at the Centre County Historical Society in State College, Pennsylvania.

"Eli Bowen Addresses His Reader" paraphrases Eli Bowen's *The Pictorial Sketch-Book of Pennsylvania* (1852), a travel guide to what he viewed as Pennsylvania's industrial wonders.

"Black Walnut" uses quotations describing the rebel yell from Ken Burns' *The Civil War* (1990).

"Jumping the Pit, Hopewell Furnace, 1936" : The italicized material comes from the editor's note to Jackson Kemper's article titled "American Charcoal Making: In the Era of the Cold-Blast Furnace" ("The Regional Review," Vol. V, No. 1, July 1940).

"Self-Portrait with Tucson": The final line quotes Ofelia Zepeda's "O'odham Dances" ("There is still a little bit of night left") from *Ocean Power* (The University of Arizona Press, 1995).

Acknowledgments

I am grateful to the editors of the following journals in which these poems first appeared:

Architrave   "Reading the Landscape"
Bayou Magazine   "Augury"
Broadsided Press   "Final Descent into Phoenix"
Cimarron Review   "Night Watch, Greenwood Furnace"
Christianity & Literature   "Waiting for the Bridegroom"
Connotation Press   "She Dreams about the Exodus," "Watershed"
Crab Orchard Review   "What the Susquehanna Tells Me about Blood"
The Hollins Critic   "Team"
Journal of Mennonite Writing   "Meditation for Polly," "And Zion Was Our Mournful Theme"
Mount Hope   "The Good Year," "Minnie Gulch, July 1998"
Nimrod International Journal   "Greener Than"
Passages North   "Self-Portrait with Tucson"
Resonance: A Theological Journal   "Wonder"
The San Pedro River Review   "Lighter"
Under a Warm Green Linden   "The Unicorn in Captivity"
Zócalo Magazine   "Even These Things Will Pass Away"
Zone 3   "Voluntary Remediation"

Thank you also to Finishing Line Press for publishing a selection of these poems in the chapbook *Jumping the Pit*.

Thank you to Andrew Saulters for giving this book a home and for his keen eye in editing it. To Robin Becker and Julia Spicher Kasdorf, I am deeply grateful for wise direction and ongoing encouragement. Thank you to the Penn State graduate writing workshops and everyone who offered feedback on the earliest of these poems. Thank you to Shelby Driscoll Salemi and Melissa Michal for comments and support. Eleanor Wilner provided necessary encouragement at just the right time. To my family, thank you all for being the most enthusiastic readers, listeners, and supporters of everything that I do. This book would not exist without Abby Minor, who first drove me past Centre Furnace, and who I thank for being an attentive reader, gentle advocate, and friend in all the years since. Loving thanks to Luke, the best companion in furnace hunting, for going there and back again.

Julie Swarstad Johnson lives in Tucson, Arizona. She is the author of the poetry chapbook *Jumping the Pit* and has served as Artist in Residence at Gettysburg National Military Park. She works at the University of Arizona Poetry Center.

Text and titles in Fournier.
Cover and interior design
by Andrew Saulters.

The author signed 26 hardbound copies,
lettered A through z. An additional 75
hardbound copies and 400 bound in paper
were produced by Unicorn Press.

Titles in the Unicorn Press First Book Series